I0087809

Praise for
Little Buddha Dog

"You will want to read this beautiful love story written by a soul whose heart speaks the language of love, beauty and wisdom. To me it's not about grief, it's about love."
  - **Dr. Marj Britt**, Senior Minister Emeritus, Unity Church of Tustin and Founder of CalledByLove.com & Institute

"This lovely little book is a wonderful teaching about the love between a person and a dog. But even more important, it is a teaching about how love is not just about caring, it is also about letting go. Read it and let your heart be touched."
  - **Daphne Rose Kingma**, Bestselling author of *The Ten Things To Do When Your Life Falls Apart*, *The Future of Love*, and *Coming Apart*

"As a veterinarian, we treasure so many moments with our patients and clients who love them. One of our greatest sorrows is to say goodbye. Rita's story about her love for Countess and her final act of caring, moved me and reminded me of how special the relationship is between pets and people."
  - **Alicia Oakley**, DVM, Doctor of Veterinary Medicine Irvine Veterinary Services

"Your story was so beautiful! It touched my heart and I just cried while reading it, especially since I lost my baby boy, Kingston, so recently. It's a very moving story that every pet parent should read after losing their pet."
  - **Andrea Wagner**, Pet Owner

Praise for
Little Buddha Dog

"This is a beautiful story of love and surrender. It will touch your heart in remembrance of the deep and unconditional love of a pet. If your life and heart have been transformed by this love, this book will be like finding a kindred spirit on the path of life."
- **Debora de la Cuesta**, LCSW, Coach, Psychotherapist & Licensed Clinical Social Worker

"Little Buddha Dog, about Countess was a wonderful read and touched my heart, bringing me to tears. My favorite quote; 'It's better to have loved and lost, than to have never loved at all'. . .Perhaps they're not stars up in heaven but the souls of our loved ones shining down on us."
 - **Tristin Shiells**, Keeper of the Animals & Pet Owner

"It has been my honor to have Rita as a client and her wonderful dog, Countess, as our patient for 14 years. If a dog and her caretaker take on the same traits, this was very true of Rita and Countess...always positive, always smiling, always happy. Throughout the circle of life, there is happiness and sadness. The special love and bond that Rita & Countess had for each other remains and lives on in the hearts and minds of all of us."
 - **Eddie Cole**, DVM, Doctor of Veterinary Medicine
 Irvine Veterinary Services

Little Buddha Dog

Little Buddha Dog

A short love story
about a woman's best friend
& their last day together

Rita Tanos

Copyright © 2012 by Rita Tanos

All Rights Reserved. This book may not be reproduced in whole or part, stored in a retrieval system, or transmitted in any form or by any means - electronic, mechanical, or other - without written permission from the publisher and author, except by a reviewer, who may quote brief passages in a review.

Library of Congress Control Number: 2012921111

Softcover ISBN: 978-0-9884074-1-1
Digital ISBN: 978-0-9884074-0-4

First printing, November 2012
Printed in the United States of America

Dedication

For Countess, my Beloved Buddha Dog - whose exquisite, unconditional Love has so gently embraced me for the last 15 years.

I am eternally grateful for your love and teachings. Your big heart and buddha soul has revealed to me once again what unconditional Love is all about . . .

Such a profound teaching, my Beloved Countess, and such a deep and forever Love we share.

Thank You!

Favorite Quotes

"He is your friend, your partner, your defender, your dog. You are his life, his love, his leader. He will be yours, faithful and true, to the last beat of his heart. You owe it to him to be worthy of such devotion."

 - Unknown

"The only creatures that are evolved enough to convey pure love are dogs and infants."

 - Johnny Depp

"Animals are closer to God than humans. They are closer to the Source. The humans are more lost in the mind forms."

 - Eckhart Tolle

Contents

Acknowledgements

My deepest thanks to the hands and hearts who delivered me here with their unwaivering love and care.

To Marj Britt whose constant encouragement and steadfast love helped me birth my first book. Your love shines in my heart as a beacon of clear light, just as your mystical teachings have brought me wings to fly with eagles.

To Adrianne Grayson for spiritual kinship, sacred witness, and whose constant abiding love has gifted me with radiant light and wisdom for so many years.

To Doctors Alicia Oakley and Eddie Cole for your exquisite care and knowing intuition during the lifetime of my Beloved Countess. You are both gifted!

To Tristin Shiells, whose tender, loving care for Countess during her final days made our journey together more graceful.

Finally, and always, my deep thanks to my mother, Ruth, for your endless Love and always being there.

Introduction

The Little Buddha Dog was written the night my Beloved Countess passed through the veils. . . She has blessed my life, every day with such exquisite, unconditional love and joy!

This little book is a gift from Countess to all animal lovers who have lost their beloved pet, or for anyone considering end of life care and their pets final needs as they approach their last days of life. Faced with the decision of how to love them best during their final passage from life to death and eternity is never easy.

Sometimes love is also about letting go. . . even when we feel our hearts are breaking in the process.   Sometimes the greatest love we can extend to our beloved pet is the final act of caring enough to say goodbye.   To release them from their suffering and knowing when to say goodbye is an act of love.   This is not about us. . . this is about the precious life of an animal we cared for and loved so deeply.   We must find the courage within ourselves to accept this final act as a gift of love, knowing in our hearts that Grace is fully present in these final moments of surrender.

As they are letting go of life, we are learning how to let go of them.   Their eyes and hearts tell us everything we need to know.   They are ready when they are ready and we must know that, lovingly.

If we are the ones bestowed with the honor of being their caretaker during their life, then we too must be worthy of such devotion at the end of their lives.   To gently ease their way out of pain and suffering is our final, courageous act of love.

May you find comfort in our love story of how we shared the last day of my Little Buddha Dog's life. It was such an honor to love her well, especially during the last moments of her life.

Little Buddha Dog. . . Countess
June 13, 1996 - April 8, 2011

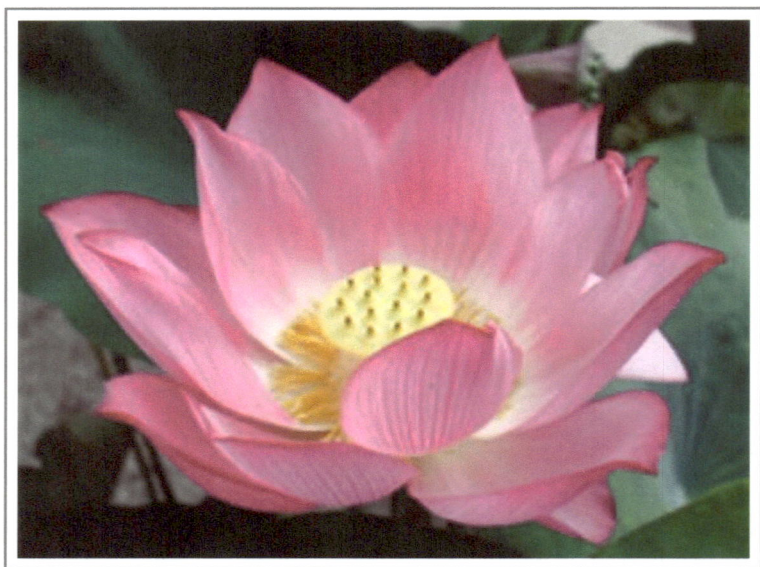

The Short Story
of
Little Buddha Dog

The soft sound of music was playing in the background as I rested my head on my Mum's lap, easing into the warm curl of her body. I think it was Vivaldi's "Four Seasons". . . very appropriate for this final page of the last chapter in my life.

I was dying slowly and Mum knew it. She tried to comfort me as best she could. . . lying here with her, at the foot of her small meditation bed, feeling the warmth of her love and the safety and protection of her soft skin and strong body.

My breathing was slow and steady, but I had become very quiet in these final days and weeks. In this present quiet moment, stillness and the soft sound of Vivaldi's violins playing in the near distance, we were in harmony with each other, my Mum and I. Her quiet breath would come in as I felt the rise of her body, and my breath would go out . . . letting go of all the cares and concerns of our little world together. Then I would breath in the life force once more, as she would breath out, and in, once again. There was grace in this simplicity. And within minutes, we both fell asleep together. I inside the caves of Mum's legs, and she, wrapped around me in a warm cocoon of love and protection. I felt safe and very loved.

And we both knew this would be the last time we would sleep together.

We drifted off, letting go of all our concerns and slid inside the sweet slumber of eternity. . . those beautiful infinite spaces where light comes inside our hearts, quiets our mind, and slowly we let go. . .into a heavenly sleep together.

When the morning light arrived, Mum took special care to give me her silken caresses. . . from the top of my head, all the way down my body and ending with my legs and four-footed paws. She let me know that no matter how rough my paw pads had felt, she loved every ounce and inch of me unconditionally, and I felt Mum's love so deeply.

I was grateful that I still had my shiny, soft and silky hair, as Mum loved to caress me and slide the palm of her hand over my body - from head to toe. My hair was still silky and smooth, and thank God Mum took the time and care to give me a bath with special shampoo in the tub, just a few weeks ago. . . After all, I am a "soft coated Wheaten Terrier", and even though I was an unusually small Wheaten, she fell in love with me the instant our eyes met, as I did with Mum.

It was an instantaneous connection of the heart space, as though we had loved and known each other before, and thank God, she could not ignore her feelings and deep, intuitive nature.

This was the beginning of our bond together. Something kept calling her back to me, and I could sense that her heart was stronger than her mind, which is why I chose her as my Mum.

Kissing her, all over her face when we met didn't make much of a difference, as her heart was already connected to mine. She was simply irresistible and funny, ever so playful, and almost as cute as I was.

And even though she was leaving the next day on a business trip to New York City and Italy for two weeks, she found a way to make it possible to adopt me! That is when I knew we would be together forever . . . She wasn't going to allow anything or anyone to come between us, now that our hearts had joined together as one heart . . . Such a Blessing!

That was just the beginning of our love and adventure together, and there were so many. . .

I almost made it to 15 years today, but I gratefully let go when Mum was finally willing to let go.

I gave her many signs that I was ready over the last two months, but she just wasn't sure. She kept asking Spirit for a sign, asking me for a sign. And because I can only speak from my heart - which is always, already silent - but fully open and alive - it took Mum a little time to tune in, and be sure I wanted to go. . . She finally got it!

Letting go is always a process. Sometimes it takes a long time, and sometimes it's in an instant of revelation . . . perhaps enlightenment in my case. You just can't help but recognize a Buddha Dog when its right in front of you!

Total stillness, utter silence and complete surrender to what is. Peace and compassion wash over me. I am letting go of it all; everything, everyone, every little bit of it . . . all of it.

So Mum slid inside the shower door, as she always does every morning, doing her yoga stretches and exercises under the steaming hot water . . . and I heard her praying to the Holy Spirit, "Sweet Beloved, give me the strength and the courage to let go completely and to accept, honor, and gracefully bow to the Sacred Presence inside of my Beloved Buddha Dog, Countess. Grace us with the knowing that our love is eternal, and let Countess know I will always be with her, now and forever more. My love for her is eternal. Our love is eternal. Show me the way. Show me how to love her well and deeply, especially on this last day of ours together."

And there we were, an hour later, strolling around the harbor, smelling the ocean air and hearing the sailboats clicking and gliding inside the bay. . . me in my pink doggie stroller Granny gifted me with last Easter (because I no longer wanted to take long walks) and Mum, who loves nature and walking, was here beside me, on our final walk together.

Mum dressed in all white this day . . . purity of all the rainbow colors she knew I would want to see on this final day of ours together. She kept trying to find a perfect spot for us to sit together, one last time, without anyone else around. The harbor was not quiet enough for

Mum, and she wanted to sit on the grass with me in her arms. So off we went again, to another side of the harbor, until Mum found the perfect patch of green grass, glistening in front of the water and sunshine, in complete silence. No one was around . . . just the two of us, and the harbor squirrels and seagulls.

So we sat, Mum and I, for a long time . . . she cried her tears and thanked me again in a million ways for all my unconditional love for her over these last 15 years . . . and I listened. I heard everything she needed to say to me. This was her way of letting go, and finally, when she went inside the silence and just surrendered to the quiet, Mum's heart met mine and we felt our Oneness with all and with each other. She felt my unconditional love for her. I felt her unconditional love for me. And we sat in the sacred silence for a long time together . . . just feeling our great love. It was so beautiful!

Slowly we arose from our meditation together, and Mum took me for a final drive in her car, and a final visit with my vet, Dr. Oakley. . . a beautiful soul and spirit who saved my life at least a couple of times over these last two years.

Mum drove to the back of the clinic, so I wasn't even sure where I was, but no matter where I was, I was ready to go . . . and I knew now that Mum finally was. We sat together for a long time in the silence, in the backseat of our car. Mum kept stroking my hair and telling me how much she loved me . . . that it was all OK and not to be afraid . . . that she would always be with me.

After a while, my life saver who was now to be my savior at the end of my life arrived in the backseat of Mum's car.   She greeted me with kindness and compassion . . . Dr. Oakley knew I was ready to pass through the veils immediately, as she sat and comforted Mum and I for a few minutes. Finally we entered the back door, near the gardens.   It was too cold to sit outside.   We entered a special room that Dr. Oakley reserved for just Mum and I.   She was so gentle and kind . . .her heart was wide open.

I took only one look at her as I leaned my head inside her arms, with Mum on the other side of me, still caressing me, still loving me, and another woman came in to greet us. . .

a technician that remembered me and had cared for me since I was baby Countess. Here she was again at the end of my life, on my final day of life, helping me once again, easing my way to a final state of peace.

How sweet! How beautiful that she remembered me as she told Mum she knew me well, since I was just a puppy.   She knew my veins, she knew all the catheters I had over the years, and right now, she knew exactly how to make it easier on me.   Here was the angel of my veins, and the director of my bliss to come.

It was Dr. Oakley that would take me there, to a final resting place of peace, when Mum said it was OK, when she knew it was better than OK. Even Uncle Eddie (Dr. Cole) came in to say his final goodbyes and tried to lighten up Mum's spirit. He didn't know what to say, but I felt his sweet heart and loving kindness. Mum felt it too and just smiled at him. She had no words . . .

I knew I was at the right place at the right time, and now it was our time, Mum and I, to finally say our final goodbye. This was a good day to die. She kept me in her warm sleeve of love and finally, I let go . . . peacefully, quietly, gently, and ever so easily . . . Mum just held me in her arms until the warmth of my body was gone. My soul began its passage through the heavenly veils in Mum's arms. I was ever so grateful!

I knew Mum would be fine. She would have the rest of her life to remember all the sweet memories of our times together . . . Such a good life! Such a good time! Such a loving Mum! Such a fun Mum! And what wonderful loving vets, taking such good care of me throughout my life . . . as and when I needed them, from birth to the end of my life.

But Mum, you are my shining light, and I thank you for letting me go when I did. Your Little Buddha Dog, your baby Countess was so tired, and so ready to pass through the veils to the other side of life. The doorway to death is the entry way to heaven. I will always be with you and you with me. Our Love is eternal. You do know that!

Thank you Mum for all your years of unconditional LOVE . . . for our JOY, our LAUGHTER, and our many fun games together! YOU have made my life so SPECIAL! Thank you for loving me the way you do! We shall float through the ethers together, into eternity with our precious, infinite LOVE.

Forever & Always, and in All Ways,

Your Little Buddha Dog . . .
Your Baby Girl (as you always called me).

Love to you Mum,

Your Countess
xoxoxoxoxoxoxo

Baby Countess & Mum

Santa Barbara, CA

Epilogue

There is no easy way to let go of a beloved pet. We carry them with us in our hearts forever. Four weeks after my Little Buddha Dog, Countess, passed through the veils, I was out for a morning walk. As I reached inside the pocket of my jeans, there were three little doggie bones stashed away from our last visit to Petsmart, one of her favorite afternoon outings. It brought an instant smile to my face! These were the last physical reminders of her, right here inside my pocket . . .

Such a delightful surprise!

Every day as I walk up and down the stairs, I pass our family portrait and am reminded of the joy we shared together for 15 years. The kiss on Granny's face makes me laugh as I remember the day we had our portrait taken at the Montage in Laguna Beach.

It took me well over a month before I could bring myself to give away her beds, bowls, collars and leashes to the homeless dogs. The collar she wore for the last year of her life was pink and filled with heart crystals. I decided to keep that one. It made me feel close to her when I held it in my hands. The last items I finally let go of were her winter coats and black, wool turtleneck sweater that Granny hand-knit for Countess. It still had her smell on it. . . and while it was hard to part with, I knew there was a living, homeless dog out there that needed it more than I did. So off it went.

What I am left with is the Love! . . . and the precious memories that live inside my heart. I am so grateful for this eternal gift of Love that lives on inside of me. There is much comfort in these wonderful memories that most often make me smile and laugh. It was my Little Buddha Dog, Countess, who was the constant heartbeat at my feet everyday, always reminding me to follow my heart. Thank God I did!

As you walk through the journey with your beloved four-footed friend, may you be comforted in their eternal Love that will always live on inside your heart!

Eyeing the Koi Fish...

Countess at the Lotus Pond

"Look within. Be Still. Free from fear and

attachment. Know the sweet joy of the way."

- Buddha

Baby Countess

Spoiled-rotten in her very chic bed!

"It is better to travel well

than to arrive."

- Buddha

Countess' Little Red Train. . .

This excited her more than anything!

With heart racing, she loved chasing it . . .

and finally got to take it for a ride!

"If you light a lamp for someone else

it will also brighten your path."

- Buddha

The Beach at Sunset. . .

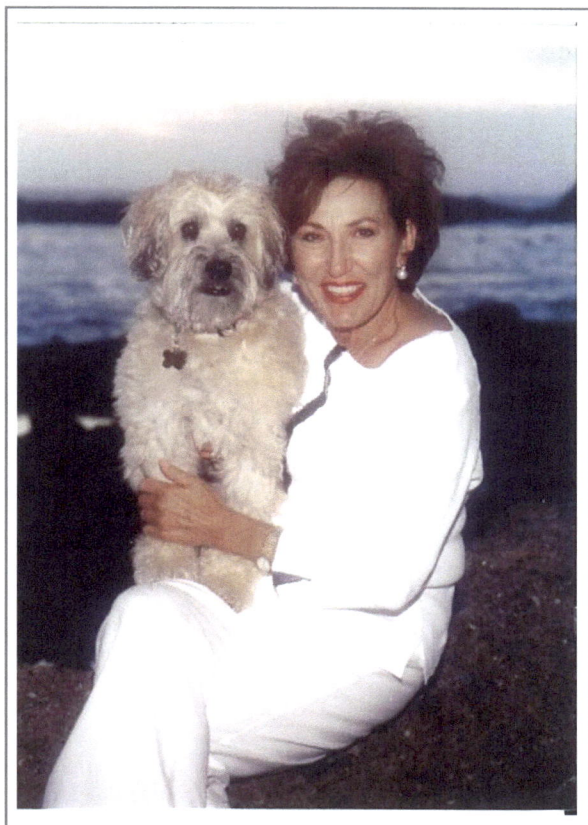

With Mum!

"Listen to the moan of a dog

for its master.

That whining is the connection.

There are love-dogs

no one knows the names of.

Give your life to be one of them."

- Rumi

Flirtatious young Countess. . .

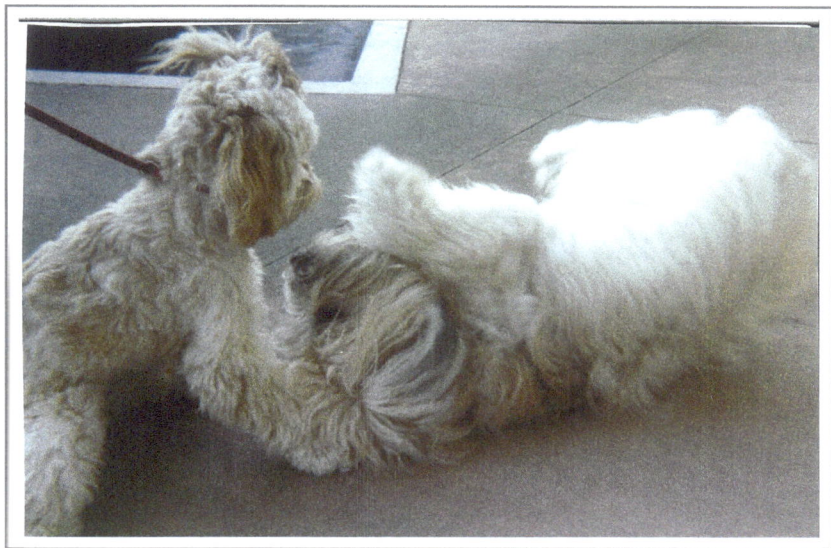

Rolling over to high-paw her Friend!

"Let the beauty we love be what we do.

There are hundreds of ways to kneel

and kiss the ground."

- Rumi

Striking a Pose. . .

Mum & I in San Juan Capistrano

"Your task is not to seek for love, but merely to seek and find all the barriers within your-self that you have built against it."

- Buddha

Baby Buddha Dog in Winter

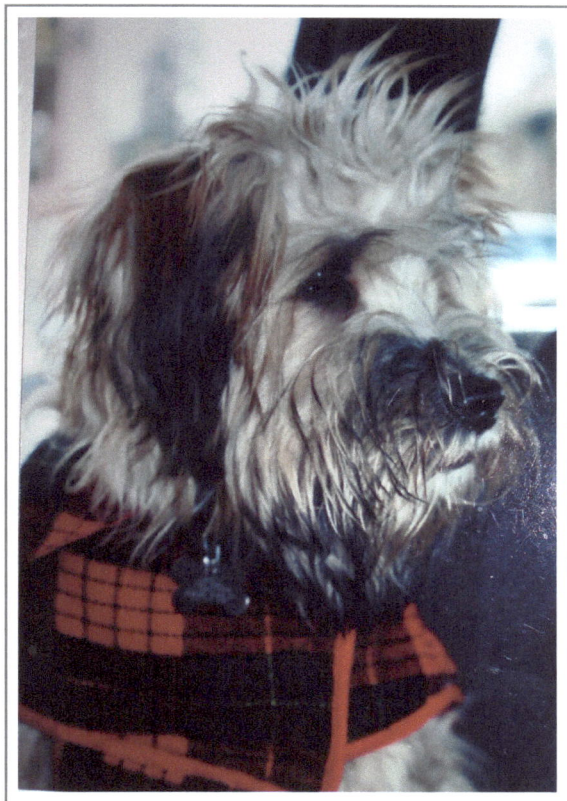

Sedona, AZ

"The greatest prayer is patience."

- Buddha

Countess hiding under the Table. . .

Waiting for those juicy scraps!

"My soul is from elsewhere . . .

I'm sure of that,

and I intend to end up there."

- Rumi

The End is sometimes the beginning. . .

"*Your work is to discover your work and then with all your heart, give yourself to it.*"

- Buddha

About the Author

Rita Tanos is an accomplished and highly-experienced leader in the world of luxury and business leadership sectors with a focus on business & product development, marketing, and public relations. With an outstanding sense of style and the ability to recognize trends, Rita translates them into business opportunities.

As head of W Magazine in the Western U.S. and Canada, Rita received the "Corporate Award for Excellence & Outstanding Achievement" as Number #1 in the company for more than a decade. Inspired by beauty and possessing a very keen eye for luxury and the finer details, Rita created a luxury product company with her own brand and designs manufactured in Italy & Paris. Bellatano Luxury Goods were sold and represented by the top 200+ leading luxury retailers and designer showrooms in the U.S. After selling her company, Rita became the Associate Publisher of a national affluent home magazine. With vast expereince in marketing, public relations, publishing, and luxury products & services, Rita created Visionary Consulting & PR in response to many requests from friends and associates in the luxury industry. From small hotels and B&B's, to travel, fashion and lifestyle, they wanted help with their marketing, creative events, and public relations. With a natural ability to visualize what's possible and co-create with the owners, Visionary Consulting provides solutions and clear objectives of the how to's, from marketing, media & PR, to design, renovation, product development and community outreach.

Contact Information

To contact or find out more information about the writings of Rita Tanos, or about the Little Buddha Dog, Countess, please visit:

www.LittleBuddhaDog.com

I'd love to continue to help you on your journey and invite you to contact me through my website. Remember that every moment shared with our beloved pets throughout their life is worth every beautiful, heartbreaking and glorious moment at the end of their lives. It is the gift of their unconditional love that continues on, inside our hearts, and that love will stay with us forever!

A Final Note: Special thanks to all the people who work so hard to rescue, foster, adopt and save homeless animals. You are the Lightworker's of the World!

www.ingramcontent.com/pod-product-compliance
Lightning Source LLC
Chambersburg PA
CBHW042120060426

42446CB00038B/11

*9 780988 407411 *